PRAYING *from the* HEART *of* HOLY CROSS SPIRITUALITY

More than one hundred years ago, Blessed Basil Moreau, a courageous, energetic, and prayerful French priest, worked hard serving God and answering the many needs of his day. The Holy Cross congregations founded in his spirit continue Moreau's work around the world in parishes, schools, colleges, universities, and in many ministries to the poor. *Praying from the Heart of Holy Cross Spirituality* shares Basil Moreau's transforming spiritual vision in accessible daily readings. This book helps us see how richly God blesses work done in his name.

Rev. Theodore M. Hesburgh, C.S.C.
President Emeritus
University of Notre Dame

Through the writings, homilies, and letters of Blessed Basil Moreau, Br. Joel has captured in a new way the spirituality of Holy Cross. With each daily mediation, readers/retreatants enter into the pastoral, practical, persuasive spirituality of Blessed Basil Moreau and the four religious congregations in the Holy Cross family.

Rev. Edwin H. Obermiller, C.S.C.
Assistant Provincial
Indiana Province of Holy Cross

This work will be a great resource for both laymen and religious in their personal lives as well as in their individual ministries. It will be great for use as a spiritual tool for prayer and reflection, not only in Holy Cross ministries, but in any Catholic institution that chooses to use it.

Terry McGaha
Director of Mission Outreach and Parent/Volunteer Programs
Notre Dame High School

These meditations invite us into a deeper awareness of the desire for union with God, leading us toward a transformation through which we become the living likeness of Jesus. This is at the heart of Moreau's spirituality—becoming so identified with our model that in some way we become another Christ.

Suellen Tennyson, M.S.C.
Congregational Leader

A 30-DAY RETREAT WITH BASIL MOREAU

PRAYING *from the* HEART *of* HOLY CROSS SPIRITUALITY

Joel Giallanza, C.S.C.

ave maria press **AmP** notre dame, indiana

Founded in 1865, Ave Maria Press is a ministry of the United States Province of Holy Cross.

www.avemariapress.com

ISBN-10 1-59471-232-8 ISBN-13 978-1-59471-232-6

Cover image © istockphoto

Cover and text design by Brian C. Conley.

Printed and bound in the United States of America.

Contents

Acknowledgments

For the first section of each day's prayer, translated excerpts from various writings of Basil Moreau—his community and personal correspondence, sermons, *Christian Education*, *Christian Meditations*, *Catechism of the Christian Life and the Religious Life* and his adaptation of Saint Ignatius of Loyola's *Spiritual Exercises*[1] have been combined, rearranged, and freely adapted into modern English, for the purposes of prayer, meditation, and reflection.

A special word of gratitude must be given to Mr. Thomas Grady, publisher at Ave Maria Press, for accepting and supporting the publication of this work, and to Mr. Robert Hamma, editorial director, for his encouragement and guidance throughout the development of this project. I especially appreciate and value Bob's editorial wisdom and expertise. Ms. Catherine M. Odell, as editor, provided the suggestions and support, encouragement and editorial counsel, perceptivity and patience,

needed to move this work from concept to completion. I
am grateful for her assistance.

This book is dedicated to all those who strive to live
in the spirit of Basil Moreau and who look to him as
an inspiration, teacher, and guide along the pathways of
their spiritual journey.

Meeting Basil Moreau

*G*iven the vast span of time covered by Christian spirituality, Basil Moreau is relatively new on the scene, having lived and worked in nineteenth-century France (1799-1873). Father Moreau founded the religious brothers, priests, and sisters of Holy Cross, beginning in 1837. Originally, Moreau envisioned these men and women as a single religious community; however, that vision was modified by circumstances and church authorities.

Today, there are four religious congregations in the Holy Cross family. The *Congregation of Holy Cross* (priests and brothers) received papal approval in 1857. By that time, the original sisters, the *Marianites of Holy Cross*, had been separated by Rome and eventually received papal approval in 1867. In 1869, the United States group of Marianites became the *Sisters of the Holy Cross* and received papal approval in 1896. Similarly, in 1886, the Canadian group of Marianites became the *Sisters of Holy Cross* and received papal approval in 1910. These four congregations look to Basil Moreau as their common founder and inspiration.

Basile Antoine Moreau, commonly referred to as Basil Moreau, was born on February 11, 1799, in a small, rural village just outside Le Mans, France. He was the ninth of fourteen children. His mother ran the family farm, and his father was a wine merchant. Moreau died in Le Mans on January 20, 1873, at the age of seventy-four. Though Moreau lived and died so close to the village where he was born, it would be wrong to assume that his world was "small." He was a man of considerable talent and boundless energy for ministry. He made friends with people in every sector of life, even those with differing political and social perspectives, because he believed they could contribute to continuing the mission that God had given him. His firm belief in the enormous potential of human nature touched and transformed the lives of many people. He was a priest and professor, scholar and spiritual director, religious founder and pioneer, educator, prolific writer, and popular preacher. His interests included education and politics, agriculture and engineering, architecture and construction, theology and art, geography and navigation, music, mathematics, and more.

Father Moreau's many gifts found expression through the ministries and services in which the brothers, priests, and sisters were engaged. Because schools and parishes had been seriously compromised, not only by the French Revolution itself, but also by the subsequent and frequently shifting governmental policies and procedures, many Holy Cross religious served in educational and parochial settings, first in France and then beyond. The needs were enormous and he responded. The institution that Father Moreau founded, Our Lady of Holy Cross, became the school of choice in Le Mans. And, throughout his life, Moreau preached parish retreats and offered sacramental assistance as his time permitted. His direct involvement in all this reflected his desire and commitment to contribute personally to the transformation of the world in which he lived.

Though his vision for the transformation of French society—and even of the world—was personal and passionate, Basil Moreau knew he could not single-handedly do all that should be done. Holy Cross came into existence in response to the urgent needs of the time. He surrounded himself with men and women of many talents who shared his commitment to selfless service. Very quickly, the Holy Cross family grew in numbers and by geography. Usually, Father Moreau would send the most capable among his colleagues—men and women on whom he relied—to lead and coordinate the missionaries in far-off lands, often never to return to France. In his passion to be of service, to provide education and the sacraments, and to alleviate suffering of any kind, he did sometimes over-extend human and financial resources. He simply trusted that God would provide, and God did. Holy Cross continued to grow.

Basil Moreau was close to people; he came to know them and to care about them personally. Even over great distances, he did what he could to stay in touch. His conversation and teaching were marked by that same intimacy. His writing and preaching had a universal appeal. They were religiously reflective and meditative, but also instructive. Readers and listeners could translate his words into daily actions. His approach was pastoral, practical, and persuasive, based on faith and filled with the conviction that God's providential presence and activity are at work always, in every dimension of life. This keen sense of providence gave Father Moreau a profound capacity for hope that sustained him through difficult and painful times with his religious communities, church authorities, and civic officials. The motto he lived by and passed on to others sums up his perspective: "Hail cross, our only hope."

This conviction that the cross, in whatever form, can be a source of life and hope was an encouraging message for those who struggled and suffered in the political, economic, and religious turmoil of post-Revolutionary France. Even more, it held the promise of transformation and affirmed the goodness and potential of human nature; a promise and an affirmation not regularly heard in a society still influenced by the remnants of Jansenism. Basil Moreau was committed to "preparing the world for better times than ours," precisely because he believed better times were possible and would indeed come if people cooperated and collaborated in making the necessary efforts and sacrifices. That he inspired so many men and women to live the same commitment was good news during bleak times. It still is. Transformation is always possible; there is always cause for hope.

Today that transformation and hope are nurtured by the religious of Holy Cross and by those who minister with them in schools and universities where a quality education is provided. It is also present in parishes and other venues that offer an extensive range of pastoral services to those in need. This Holy Cross spirituality can be found in hospitals and clinics and in a variety of other ministries that respond to the pressing needs of society and the church. That response is evident through the presence and ministry of the family of Holy Cross in France, Italy, the United States, Canada, Mexico, Haiti, Peru, Chile, Brazil, Kenya, Uganda, Mali, Ghana, India, Bangladesh, and the Philippines. The women and men of Holy Cross reflect the richness and diversity of all these cultures.[2]

For Father Moreau, the spiritual life—indeed all of life—was meant to be "gravitation toward God," propelled by "a fervent and continuous desire" to be one with God. As that gravitational pull grows stronger, as the desire intensifies, transformation happens. This is good news, for any time, in any life situation. It is worthy of our confidence. Basil Moreau's instruction is straightforward, "Be convinced that nothing should shake the confidence of those who have the Lord for their portion and support." This conviction is a choice that must be made.

Whatever similarities and differences there may be between the world that Basil Moreau confronted and the world in which we live, transformation is a challenge we must accept if we are serious about our relationship with God, and sincere in our efforts toward spiritual growth. Transformation will be shaped by our faith. It will shape our future as individuals and as a people. An even deeper challenge lies in our willingness to take up the transformation because we know we must, we are convinced it is possible, and we believe that God is with us always. The choice to transform life is ours.

Living Holy Cross Spirituality

---

*B*asil Moreau passed on a rich and enduring heritage to the religious family of Holy Cross and to all those associated with Holy Cross through life and ministry. In fact, this gift has been a tremendous blessing for the entire Church—especially since his beatification on September 15, 2007.

The Moreau heritage is a challenging call to transformation; it is a heritage to be lived so that the message and mission of Jesus can continue. It is an incarnational heritage that can be recognized primarily in the context of daily life and in the faithful striving to live and love as Jesus did. Here we find little theory and mostly practice. As Father Moreau understood it, personal transformation has significant apostolic implications; it is nothing less than the catalyst for the transformation of our world. As he said, this was the primary way in which "to prepare for better times than ours." If taken up faithfully, that preparation would be the prelude to realization.

This heritage is born of the charism of Holy Cross, that distinctive gift given to Basil Moreau and continued by all those sharing his legacy. That charism is to revitalize Christian faith, to regenerate society, and to realize those "better times" by responding to the most pressing needs in our society and our world.

How do we live this heritage? How do we take up this revitalization, regeneration, and realization? What guides our response? What are the basic elements of Holy Cross spirituality for daily life? Four elements will be highlighted here.

Conforming to Christ

The first element is "Conforming to Christ." Every dimension of our personal lives must reflect the example and teaching of Jesus. This is the solid foundation upon which all transformation is built. Father Moreau writes, "Christianity is nothing else than the life of Jesus Christ reproduced in our conduct." Such conformity is not confined to special occasions or periodic events. It must pervade our entire day, every day. Because this conformity must be complete, there are no exceptions. Moreau teaches us in one of his sermons,

> In whatever interior dispositions you may be and in whatever life situation you may find yourself, look at your Model and apply yourself to imitating him; be assured that in doing so you will be perfect and you will have a sure guarantee of your salvation; because our movement toward glory depends on our resemblance to Jesus Christ.

This imitation, this conformity, is the basis of Holy Cross spirituality.

Trusting in Providence

The second element is "Trusting in Providence." The work of Providence and the call to trust in Providence appear on almost every page of Basil Moreau's writings. This was one of his most profound convictions. It remained unshaken regardless of the dilemmas or disasters that confronted him. "Divine providence has given us too many motives for encouragement and consolation for me to refrain from asking you to join with me in thanksgiving, and to leave your whole future in God's hands without anxiety over the things which take up the time of those who are of the world." Whether he had to deal with disappointments in ministries, lost opportunities, financial setbacks, or even unexpected deaths among the members, he was convinced that God had been, is now, and will continue to guide and bless us. Our task is to be attentive to the many ways that God's will can be revealed in daily life. He assures us,

> I am convinced that Providence, which has in the past done everything necessary for the development and perfection of its work, will continue to bestow on us the most abundant blessings. To insure this, we must be constantly animated by the spirit of zeal and generosity which so holy an undertaking requires. We must place all our confidence in the Lord.

We have cause for such confidence because God is always present and active among us.

Being United

The third element is "Being United." None of this is taken up in isolation from others. Our union and cooperation with others are more than camaraderie; they are a powerful force for transformation. In his very first

letter to the community Father Moreau wrote, "To succeed in the important undertaking entrusted to us, we
must be, first all, so closely united in charity as to form
one mind and one soul."

In another letter he said that our union is "a powerful lever with which we can move, direct, and sanctify
the whole world." This union is not a luxury; it is an urgent necessity. We must take the prophetic stance that
simple differences need not degenerate into sharp divi-
sions. Very early in its history, Holy Cross became inter-
national through its presence and in its personnel. It was
necessary to work together as one if anything was to be
accomplished effectively in continuing the mission and
living the gospel. So it must be today. Through daily life,
we must demonstrate the truth that it is possible for people of different perspectives and politics, languages and
lifestyles, cultures and colors to live and work together. The choice to work for unity is ours. Father Moreau
wrote,

> Let us stand in closely united ranks and, far
> from separating and scattering, let us live in
> such a manner that, as it sees the members
> of our family, the world may say of us as it
> was said of the first Christians: 'See how they
> love one another!' This is the most ardent
> desire of my heart.

Unity is a gift that the heritage of Holy Cross can bring to the world.

Hoping in the Cross

The fourth element is "Hoping in the Cross." Each of the preceding elements, and all of them together will lead to the cross, even as events of Jesus' own life led him to the cross. Basil Moreau was blunt about this. "In vain shall we seek any way leading to heaven other than the road to Calvary." This is a fundamental tenet of Christianity and a consequence of following Jesus of Nazareth. Moreau challenges us to hope in the cross because he knows it is a blessing that will lead to new life. The motto he gave to Holy Cross is *Ave Crux, Spes Unica*, "Hail cross, our only hope." It expresses his confidence in the promise of that new life.

In 1857, when he visited Canada (Montreal) and the United States (New York, Notre Dame, Philadelphia), he offered some reflections to the community members in Canada that articulate well his understanding of the place of the cross in the spiritual life, and in the heritage of Holy Cross. He explained,

> In following Jesus we are sure of reaching heaven. To follow him, however, it is

> necessary to deny ourselves and carry the cross. If we carry our cross after Jesus we will live. Life is in the cross and no place else. But we must not only take up the cross, we must carry it with courage. If we drag it after us, if we abandon it after having taken it up, if we trample it underfoot, it will not save us. Human life is a long way of the cross. It is not necessary to enter the chapel or the church to run over the various stations. The way of the cross is everywhere and we walk along it every day in spite of ourselves and often unknown to us. After all, what else should we desire since there is no other way to reach heaven.

The cross holds the promise of transformation to new life; we must embrace it.

The elements of Holy Cross spirituality—"Conforming to Christ," "Trusting in Providence," "Being United," and "Hoping in the Cross"—are much more than theological constructs or clever theories. They constitute a way of life that will be nurtured by personal and communal prayer, and specifically lived out through our own vocations and commitments. This Holy Cross way of life continues the mission of Jesus. So, it contributes to revitalizing faith, regenerating society, and realizing the "better times" that our world desperately needs and awaits. Evidently, this can only be, as Basil Moreau himself consistently said, "not a human work, but God's very own."

Using This Book for Prayer

This book is a tool for nurturing the spirit of prayerfulness—that spirit through which our attentiveness to God becomes second nature. It is also the spirit through which we recognize that we are always living in God's loving presence. As a tool, the book can be used most effectively as a complement to your usual, personal discipline of daily prayers and spiritual practices. It is not meant to replace those prayers and practices, but to support and enhance them. The contents are designed to serve as a framework for your day—every day for a month. Each daily reflection is divided into three sections.

The first section, "Awakening to God's Presence," can be used in the morning or whenever your day begins. This section focuses on a theme or principle that was of particular importance to Basil Moreau. The reflections are translated adaptations of Moreau's own words. The spirit marking these meditations is awareness, a sensitivity to God's presence and activity that will pervade whatever unfolds during your day. In a moment of interior and exterior quiet, before the busyness of the day begins, read through this section.

Read slowly through the section, line by line. Let these words sink into your heart. See and hear the words. Remember that spiritual reading is not speed-reading. The key is to approach the text, not as informational, but as inspirational. What do these reflections say to your heart? If a word, phrase, or image is particularly striking while you are reading, remain with that for a moment before moving on. As Father Moreau recommends, you will want to benefit from whatever God may be saying to you. In praying this section, you can reflect on what it says to you and how it could support you throughout the day.

The second section, "Living by God's Grace," is a single sentence. It can be used as an antiphon or mantra throughout the day. It is a quick and simple reminder of God's role in your daily life, and of what you can do to live in union with God in the midst of your everyday tasks and responsibilities. This sentence can be a challenge that you set before yourself several times a day. It may be helpful to write this phrase on a piece of paper and keep it in sight, or save it on your electronic calendar or daily planner. Then, you can readily call it to mind each time you review or revise your schedule.

The third section, "Acknowledging God's Gifts," can be used in the evening or whenever you conclude your day and prepare to rest. It is presented as a prayer to close your day. The spirit of this prayer is longing. It also recognizes the many blessings that God has given to you and to all of us. It voices a desire that those blessings continue to grace our lives. This section bolsters our commitment to live those blessings for the next day and beyond. That recognition, desire, and commitment constitute an expression of profound gratitude to God for the gift of being called to live as a follower of Jesus. As with the first section, you should set aside a period of quiet and stillness.

Take some deep breaths so that your body can share in that stillness. Read the prayer slowly, reflectively, line by line. Really hear the words as they are prayed. Then, recall and review the day's events, through memory images if possible. That way, your prayer is linked with and becomes a blessing for whatever transpired during the day. Conclude the prayer and welcome the rest that will refresh you for tomorrow.

All three sections should be adjusted to use whenever it is most practical and convenient for you. In today's world, a variety of activities configure and constitute our daily routines. The times for reflection may have to change from day to day, depending upon your schedule.

Don't worry about that. The key is fidelity so that your entire day is touched by prayer.

As Father Moreau taught and emphasized, union with God is nurtured by an increasing fidelity to prayer. The purpose of these reflections and prayers is to guide you ever more deeply toward the transformation to which Basil Moreau invites us. It is a transformation through which we clearly reflect and truly become the living likeness of Jesus.

This book can also be used randomly and spontaneously, without following the thirty-day pilgrimage from Day One to Day Thirty. There is a progression of themes through these days that reflects Moreau's perspective on the spiritual life. But, any day or combination of days can be used to focus your prayer in response to a particular need or experience. The following list indicates the themes associated with each day.

Days 1–3	Providence, recognizing God's constant presence and activity
Days 4–5	Faith, responding to God's Providence
Day 6	Holiness, living in fidelity to Providence
Days 7–9	Mission, serving others

Days 10–12	Prayer, supporting our life and mission
Days 13–14	Union, working together in the mission and with a sense of family
Days 15–17	Love, sustaining our union with one another
Days 18–21	Imitating Jesus, striving to live and love as he did
Days 22–23	Spiritual journey, progressing toward union with God through daily life
Days 24–26	Cross, embracing the transformation it offers
Day 27	Hope, watching for the Lord's return
Day 28	Gifts of the Holy Spirit, nurturing your spiritual life and mission
Day 29	Transformation, accepting the new life to which God calls you
Day 30	Mary, looking to your model and guide

Allow these themes to mix and interact with your spirit. Reflecting on and praying with a combination of these themes may also enhance your spiritual journey. The goal is to use this book in any way that will strengthen your relationship with God. It is meant to sustain your progress in living the example of Jesus.

Beyond what is presented here, Father Moreau has some wise recommendations for enhancing the quality of even your most familiar prayers. He said,

> Reflect sometimes on each word of your ordinary prayers but do not move from one word to another unless the spirit and the heart have nothing more to say and until you have drawn some practical consequence from it. At other times, stop for a second on each word of the prayer you have chosen, then penetrate into the meaning of the expression you are saying. Conclude with a personal, spontaneous prayer. These ways of praying are very useful for avoiding routine and they awaken our attentiveness to prayers that we are accustomed to using.

Finally, this book can be used for group reflection and sharing. There is a communal dimension within the transformation to which we are called. We can encourage, support, and challenge one another along the spiritual journey. The second section of each day, "Living by God's Grace," can be useful for a communal reflection and sharing. It could inspire practical strategies for making the day's simple instructions a reality in daily life.

However this book is used, may it nurture within you a "fervent and continuous desire" for God. That, Father Moreau said, is the very nature of prayer. That desire is an essential element of the spiritual life. If this book makes even a small contribution in that regard, then it will fulfill the noblest of tasks.

A 30-Day Retreat
with Basil Moreau

Day One

AWAKENING TO GOD'S PRESENCE

Live a balanced life,
for neither
discouragement nor pride
serves us well.
And neither
truly reflects who we are.
God is more gentle with us
than we are with ourselves.
God balances
ups and downs,
the good times
with the not-so-good times.
We could become
too proud
if all those around us
were admirers.
And disheartening
would be our lot
if all were critics.
We need
a discerning ear,
a listening heart,

a sense of balance
and humor.
We should not
expect only good times
and eschew the bad.
The important point
is to do everything
and accept everything
in conformity
to God's will.

LIVING BY GOD'S GRACE

Be gentle as God is gentle.

ACKNOWLEDGING GOD'S GIFTS

May this night's rest
be filled
with the peace and quiet
that will refresh
my efforts for tomorrow.
Accept this day, God,
and all it held for me.
Make holy tomorrow
and whatever it may bring.

Help me to live
the grace of balance,
seeing and celebrating
your will
ever around me,
guiding me,
beckoning me.
I want to live that grace.
For this day, thank you.
Bless this night.
May tomorrow be a fresh beginning.

Day Two

Make good use
of today.
In fact,
make the best use of it.
Time will not wait,
and this day—
as all of life—
will pass.
We can look behind us
at days gone by.
They can appear
as little more than
shadows passing,
or as drops into the ocean.
But we have today.
Seize it, use it,
and contribute
to making God's will
a part of the present moment,
every moment.
That won't be easy.
We need courage for now,

and hope for a better life,
for ourselves
and for everyone else.
If we accept today
the future is ours too.
Keep your eyes,
hands, and hearts
fixed on both.

LIVING BY GOD'S GRACE

Be courageous and hopeful.

ACKNOWLEDGING GOD'S GIFTS

May this night's rest
give me
energy and enthusiasm
for tomorrow and beyond.
I give you, Lord,
what I have done today.
Weave it with
your will for me
and for the world.
Let me take up tomorrow
with conviction,

courage, and confidence.
Let me make a difference.
I want to make a difference.
For this day, thank you.
Bless this night.
May tomorrow be a fresh beginning.

Day Three

God does guide our lives,
and for that
we can be thankful.
God does bless our lives.
With gratitude,
we invite even more blessings.
Just because
we don't always see
the guidance or the blessings
does not mean
they are absent.
It doesn't mean
that God neglects us.
It only means that
we do not see the
guidance and blessings.
We must believe
that God always guides,
blesses, and loves us.
Our life today
and our life's work
every day

belong to God.
We are God's work.
Our plans and our efforts
are more than
a human combination
of energy and accomplishment.
They are graced reflections
of God who is ever with us.

LIVING BY GOD'S GRACE

Believe that God is always present and active.

ACKNOWLEDGING GOD'S GIFTS

May this night's rest
refresh my eyes
and my heart
to look and listen
for God's work
within and around me.
Accept the day that has passed
with its moments
when I was aware of you,
and also when I forgot to notice.
For tomorrow, Lord, remind me anew

of your caring and your love.
Heal any unbelief in me
so that I may become
a guide and blessing
for others.
I want to believe.
For this day, thank you.
Bless this night.
May tomorrow be a fresh beginning.

Day Four

Have you ever
cut a limb from a tree
or a branch from a plant?
Even in the driest weather,
you may have noticed the moisture,
the juices, the sap that maintain life
and nurture its growth.
Blood does the same for us,
and for all in the animal world.
Being a liquid,
it takes our shape.
It moves with us
and keeps us alive.
Such is faith for the soul.
It is food for the soul,
nourishment for the heart.
It gives shape to our daily lives.
We can exist without it,
only as a biological entity.
But to be human,
to know that we are created
in God's image and likeness,

to reach the potential
that creation holds for us,
we need faith.
The limb and the branch
wither apart from their sustaining sap.
We will wither without faith.
With faith, we flourish
and so live for God and with God
in everything we do.

LIVING BY GOD'S GRACE

Act as one created in God's image and likeness.

ACKNOWLEDGING GOD'S GIFTS

May this night's rest
revitalize my faith
and my conviction
that I am God's creation.
I am imperfect, but precious.
I am incomplete, but developing.
Take this day, God,
and grace it in my memory
as a ready reminder
of my growth in days to come.

Help me to continue on my way
tomorrow—and during the days that follow.
Help me to know who you are, and
to know who I am.
Teach me to live in the beauty of both.
I want to reflect God.
For this day, thank you.
Bless this night.
May tomorrow be a fresh beginning.

Day Five

What identifies us? Really?
How do people know
who we are?
What we value?
Where our lives are going?
Reflecting on life teaches us
that identity is not
as stable as it may seem
if we build it upon
appearances and accomplishments.
Once these things shift
or disappear altogether,
we reconfigure our identities.
We think or wish that they
could be more durable, fixed
for today and for all time.
Faith can shape our identities
if we allow it to do that.
Faith gives us conviction
about God's truth and love for us.
Faith gives us power
to act on that truth and love.

Faith is alive.
It penetrates our hearts deeply
and passes into our hands deftly.
And so, it makes a difference in our world.
Where there is faith, there is life.
It touches all of life,
for our whole life.
It affects even the least details of everyday life.
Others will see that.
What identifies us? Really?

LIVING BY GOD'S GRACE

Identify with faith and live by faith.

ACKNOWLEDGING GOD'S GIFTS

May this night's rest
give me the quiet and distance I need
from the many things
that pressure me.
Those things beg for my attention and acquiescence,
pulling me, vying for my time,
trying to define who I am.
Lord, grace this day now ending.
Draw it into your gentle mercy.

Let me hold to whatever good I have done
for the benefit of others, and
for the glory of your name.
As tomorrow's dawn arrives,
keep me focused on you, and
on those I love and serve.
Strengthen my faith.
I want to be all that you have created me to be.
For this day, thank you.
Bless this night.
May tomorrow be a fresh beginning.

Day Six

This business
of trusting and believing,
of striving to be holy—
and dare we say—trying to be perfect
is very hard work.
How to begin and sustain holiness?
Where to look for guidance?
What is the standard?
When will we arrive there?
The questions can multiply and blur into oblivion.
The demands of daily life
reassert themselves with urgency,
demanding our undivided attention.
We can come to believe
that holiness and perfection
are simply beyond our reach.
However long we journey,
we just won't make it.
But God didn't make it this difficult.
We made it difficult over time, over the centuries.
We pile expectations on top of assumptions,
creating impossible standards and scenarios.

God does not attach our perfection to any of that.
God looks to the little stuff in everyday life.
The small acts of kindness and generosity,
a wave, a smile, a welcome,
a helping hand and a gentle word.
This is what God sees.
Holiness and perfection are well within our grasp.
We just need to live today the best we can,
using what we have right in our hands and hearts.

LIVING BY GOD'S GRACE

Embrace today as God's invitation to holiness.

ACKNOWLEDGING GOD'S GIFTS

May this night's rest
clear my head and my heart
of those unattainable standards I have set.
Those goals only weary my hands,
and discourage my efforts.
They drain me of energy for the future.
Transfigure the day that is closing, God.
Let me cherish it and take from it
whatever I will need
to live well in the days ahead.

Let me begin anew tomorrow,
noticing the beauty and potential
of the tiniest happenings.
I want to relish and rejoice
in the opportunities they present.
I want the holiness and perfection meant for my life.
For this day, thank you.
Bless this night.
May tomorrow be a fresh beginning.

Day Seven

We take up our tasks and work.
We do what we have to do,
and what we can do for the good
of our families,
and for the benefit of others.
It is all part of who we are
as humans, as people of God.
But we need not work alone.
God accompanies us, works with us,
guides us, loves us.
Even more, by grace,
God initiates our work
and brings it to completion.
Our work is truly God's own.
This is not automatic,
as if the transformation of our world
could come without our attention,
involvement, and care.
Through our tasks and work,
we clear a path for God's work.
We do this by removing obstacles
and taking up our responsibilities

to the best of our ability.
Such is our mission.
We must do what God does
so that God can work through us and with us
for the good of others.

Living by God's Grace

Contribute to continuing God's work.

Acknowledging God's Gifts

May this night's rest
renew my sense of purpose,
my willingness to be
part of God's own continuing mission.
Fold the work I have done this day
deep into the power of your grace.
May it bear fruit for good,
even if I do not know when, and
even if I do not understand how.
Sharpen my resolve for tomorrow
to be a contributor
in your plans for this world.
Keep me faithful to my efforts, Lord.
I trust that your work and your will

can be accomplished through them.
I want to continue your mission.
For this day, thank you.
Bless this night.
May tomorrow be a fresh beginning.

Day Eight

Living well takes commitment and
not just a casual promise.
We need a vibrant dedication to values.
Living well as Christians
takes a commitment to the mission.
This mission is clear:
we must extend the knowledge,
teaching, and love of Jesus Christ
in the hearts of all people.
Mission is a matter of the heart.
Knowledge and insight are needed,
but the lasting work, the Gospel work
of building and sustaining a culture of love
must be spread from heart to heart.
Mission will be compromised
if the mind is cultivated
at the expense of the heart.
The result would be machine-like efficiency.
Meanwhile, the heart would atrophy
and love would thereby be diminished.
We need to work in the mission together,
united with one another.

This mission is communal in nature.
If we can be one in this,
we can transform our world.
Everyone's gifts are needed for the work.
Our vocation to continue what Jesus began
is the work of each and all.
In the eyes of God and the people,
we are responsible for that mission,
individually and collectively.
This is the commitment needed for living well,
and we will have to give an accounting.

LIVING BY GOD'S GRACE

Work together with others in advancing the mission
of Jesus.

ACKNOWLEDGING GOD'S GIFTS

May this night's rest
nurture within me a revitalized commitment
to all that I am as a Christian.
Accept my work of this day
as a part of the mission,
however small it may have been
and even if I did not see or sense it.

Let me continue my journey tomorrow,
confident of your presence within me, Lord.
Help me to be convinced of your guidance,
and confirmed by your grace.
Help me to recognize all those
who can assist and accompany me.
Lead me to all those for whom I can do the same.
Let us complete the work you've given us—
making your reign, the reign of God, a reality.
I want to work with others in preparing for God's reign.
For this day, thank you.
Bless this night.
May tomorrow be a fresh beginning.

Day Nine

Mission is more than meets the eye.
Hard work is involved, yes;
but it is not just about activity.
Mission and our parts in it
involve relationship, first of all.
It is all about love,
love for God, love for others.
That love is a passionate desire
to make God known, loved, and served.
We long to be models of love for others.
That is the relationship,
that is the hard work.
Such desire is to love God,
to esteem what we do,
and to care about others.
That describes the goal of our words and our actions.
Fulfilling that desire
makes us strong and gentle.
Our strength is courage and fidelity
in the face of difficulties and trials.
Our gentleness reflects the nature of God,
speaking and acting through us.

We can and must be part of such a mission.
Why? Because we are called,
because we are graced, and
because God loves us.
We must be part of this mission
because we want to be holy.
Mission is more than meets the eye.
It can be a tricky business.
But then, so is love.

LIVING BY GOD'S GRACE

Bring love into every action, every situation, every moment.

ACKNOWLEDGING GOD'S GIFTS

May this night's rest
re-ignite my desire
to love God above all else.
I want to proclaim that love
through all my actions,
however small or simple they may be.
Make up, by your grace,
for any lack and lapse
in my willingness to love today.

Please pardon me for the moments
when I chose not to love.
God, let me love anew tomorrow,
so that I may be known by love.
Whatever I do or say,
may it be your action and your word.
Through me, may others know you are near.
I want to love God and to make God known, loved,
served.
For this day, thank you.
Bless this night.
May tomorrow be a fresh beginning.

Day Ten

We need to pray every day,
not because someone said so,
or because some law demands it.
We need to pray
because we love God, and
because we want to be blessed.
Prayer is a relationship,
built by love.
It is attained through union of hearts;
it is sustained with fidelity.
Think of prayer, imagine prayer
as a sort of gravitation toward God.
Whether slow or fast,
steady or frenetic,
the direction remains the same.
Our lives move toward God
when we decide to pray,
whatever the pace or practice we use.
We encourage this gravitation
by talking to God frequently.
Just speaking God's name
can express our love and our longing.

We cooperate with the gravitational pull
by calling to mind God's presence
working within, around, and through us.
We consent to this force of gravity
by exploring our motives and actions,
seeing if they match our faith.
Prayer heightens our awareness of God.
Prayer strengthens us for the mission.
We need to pray every day.

LIVING BY GOD'S GRACE

Determine how and when to pray today.

ACKNOWLEDGING GOD'S GIFTS

May this night's rest
sharpen my eyes to see you.
May it clear my ears to hear you,
and lead my heart to love you.
Accept the day now passing
as a prayer of longing.
May this prayer be one with you now,
and in the days yet to dawn.
For tomorrow, Lord, teach me to pray
even as you taught your disciples.

Take my words to you
and my thoughts of you,
however disconnected or incomplete they may be.
Accept my earnest attempts to praise you,
acknowledge you, love you.
I want to be a person of prayer.
For this day, thank you.
Bless this night.
May tomorrow be a fresh beginning.

Day Eleven

Jesus taught us to pray:
"Your will be done on earth as in heaven."
A simple enough teaching to hear,
more complicated to follow.
Human nature can be such that
we seek our own will, our own way,
by preference over all others, even God's.
Our will is not bad,
but on its own
it cannot go the distance.
It cannot heal our weaknesses
or fulfill our aspirations.
The sacrifice of our will
and our obedience to God's will
are a source of strength,
a pledge of hope,
and a promise of salvation.
In God's will,
darkness is dispelled,
light is born,
and we are inclined toward
discipline, humility, love.

In God's will, we can be transformed
to live something of heaven's life,
even now, even here.
We would desire nothing but God.
All our actions would be shaped by that desire.
We just need to will all this,
guided by grace, nourished by prayer.
Let us pray—and live—
as Jesus taught us.

LIVING BY GOD'S GRACE

Pursue and practice God's will.

ACKNOWLEDGING GOD'S GIFTS

May this night's rest
give me a needed break
from my own will.
I need relief from its demands and expectations,
its assumptions and tendencies.
Bless this day that is closing, Lord.
Let me recall those times when you
called and waited for my
acknowledgment and assent.
When tomorrow dawns, show me your will.

Grant me the grace, courage, and love
to embrace it and do it.
Help me to trust that it will lead me
to salvation and union with you.
I want to know and do God's will.
For this day, thank you.
Bless this night.
May tomorrow be a fresh beginning.

Day Twelve

Jesus taught us to pray:
"Give us, today, our daily bread."
It is a simple enough request to make,
but it is complex in its meaning.
Bread is basic, uncomplicated, necessary,
replenishing our energy after work,
fulfilling fundamental human needs.
Bread helps us to focus.
We come across many distractions
along the byways of our journey.
They can delay us and divert us
from the directions we should take.
We need not clutter our prayer with them.
We ask for bread, for what will sustain life
and help us to continue to grow.
We ask for God's grace
since we cannot provide for ourselves.
If we ask from the heart, God will respond.
We ask for all this today and every day
to remind us that we need not be anxious
about tomorrow and our future.
God's providence will care for us.

The providence that strengthens us today
will give us the good we need every day.
Let us learn what to ask for,
this day, and in the time to come.
Let us learn to know the bread
and the blessings promised to us.
We must accept the bread that is given,
offered by grace, recognized through prayer.
Let us pray—and live—
as Jesus taught us.

LIVING BY GOD'S GRACE

Seek the bread that God gives today.

ACKNOWLEDGING GOD'S GIFTS

May this night's rest
be nourishment and refreshment
for my body and my heart.
May it give me strength and stamina
for the days to come.
God, take the day now past
and let me be blessed
by the possibilities it had.
Keep alive the promises it held,

even if I missed or ignored them.
Tomorrow will be a new day,
bringing yet more bread.
Give me another opportunity,
granting me a share in your life,
guiding me closer to you.
I want to taste and see the bread that God provides.
For this day, thank you.
Bless this night.
May tomorrow be a fresh beginning.

Day Thirteen

Each dawn heralds a new day,
a beginning, a fresh start.
And yet, each new day is a continuation,
a chance to contribute once again,
an opportunity to make a difference.
By faith we are all construction workers
in this great adventure of living the Gospel.
We are building the reign of God.
The foundations have been well laid
by those who have gone before us.
Our efforts continue the work already begun.
They are part of this gradual effort.
Some day, it will be completed
even though we may not see it.
We cannot do everything,
but we must do something.
Each worker has a contribution to make
from experience and the expertise of personal skill.
The stones and steps, the wood and wiring
are prepared and arranged and set in place
to enhance the beauty of the whole building.
Cooperation and collaboration, born of union,

will assure success in the project.
It is no different for God's work—the work of
charity that is our Christian vocation.
Union is a powerful lever.
We can move, direct, and sanctify the whole world,
provided we don't allow any form of evil to interfere.
We are workers in constructing the Gospel life.
We must work with one another to succeed.

LIVING BY GOD'S GRACE

Cooperate and collaborate with others.

ACKNOWLEDGING GOD'S GIFTS

May this night's rest
heighten my awareness
of the gifts, talents, and skills
I have the privilege of sharing with others.
Deepen my desire to use all my capabilities
as an expression of my faith in you, God.
Deepen my hope in this world's potential for good.
For the day now closing,
let the efforts I have made
be part of your own presence and activity.
Let me be a part of transforming this world

and preparing it for all you have promised.
For tomorrow, may I be selfless and generous
in sharing whatever I can, whenever I can.
I want to work with others for the good of all.
I want to offer all I am and do for the world's
transformation.
For this day, thank you.
Bless this night.
May tomorrow be a fresh beginning.

Day Fourteen

AWAKENING TO GOD'S PRESENCE

Being family, being united with others
really begins with the small things,
those simple interactions, often dismissed,
as too ordinary to hold meaning.
Practicing little courtesies
and mutual acts of politeness
in our encounters and discussions
goes a long way in building unity.
Jesus recommended love above all else.
That requires practice in everything,
at all times and everywhere.
After love for God, our love for others
is the second great commandment,
and the root of all true union.
There are big blessings, too,
in being family and being united.
It is good to seek reconciliation immediately,
avoiding selfishness, jealousy, prejudice, pride.
The effects of this will be quickly evident.
We will develop for one another
great respect, sincere esteem,
and cordial affection, just like friends do.

Think of what that would do for our world!
Living our faith unites our efforts.
And, the oneness of those efforts
tends toward that perfect union of hearts
which is the bond and strength of all we do.
Our union with one another,
if it is to be real, if it is to last,
must be from the heart and fulfilled in the heart.

LIVING BY GOD'S GRACE

Work at being one with others.

ACKNOWLEDGING GOD'S GIFTS

May this night's rest
deepen my longing
for union in our world.
Even more, may it strengthen
my desire to be a means of unity,
reconciliation, and peace among people.
Bless what I have done this day.
Let it be a part, however small,
of your plan to bring all into union with you.
Jesus, you prayed that your followers be one.
May your prayer find fulfillment through me.

Tomorrow will be a new day
and will bring new opportunities
to make this world a better place,
a place worthy of a loving God.
I want to be a part of building that place.
For this day, thank you.
Bless this night.
May tomorrow be a fresh beginning.

Day Fifteen

We must love others
because, like us,
they are created in
God's own image and likeness.
We must love others
because our God is their God too,
and God wants us to love them.
This was the most important lesson
that Jesus Christ gave to us.
As he said, this is the only way
people would really know
that we are serious about following him.
We must love others
even as we love ourselves.
Our self-love may be sincere and constant;
still, Jesus remains our model.
Examine Jesus' love for others.
Love marked his whole life,
especially in the way he presented himself
and in his patience with others.
He gave whatever he had to offer
to all who needed him.

His love, kindness, and attentiveness
extended to all, without distinction.
He cared for everyone,
and did good even to those against him.
We may not have the same affection
for enemies as for friends.
But, we must not exclude them from our prayer,
and we must pardon them.
This is the love to which we are called.

LIVING BY GOD'S GRACE

Study Jesus' love for others.

ACKNOWLEDGING GOD'S GIFTS

May this night's rest
deepen my understanding
of Jesus' way to love others,
that I might care for them and encourage them
on their way to union with God.
Lord, thank you for this day,
for those who love and care for me,
and for those I have the privilege to love.
May I see that I am worthy of love,
and growing in my capacity to love.

Tomorrow will come quickly
with its flood of people and situations.
Give me patience with them.
Fill me with kindness and a spirit of helpfulness.
Let me love them.
I want to be Jesus' presence for others.
For this day, thank you.
Bless this night.
May tomorrow be a fresh beginning.

Day Sixteen

Jesus called us to love.
That's not a theory.
In fact, it's hard work.
Love must be many things to be real.
Love is:
Patient.
So, we accept whatever burdens
come to us from others,
without burdening them in return.
Kind.
That makes us honest,
considerate, pleasant, and
having an openness to all.
Encouraging.
So, we are not to be envious or jealous of others'
good fortune.
Rather, we wish them every blessing, and hope for
even greater fortune for them.
Pure.
We are attentive to self and others.
We attend to ourselves so that any tone of voice or
gesture

that would offend can be avoided.
We pay attention to others so we can know
what might hurt them and stay clear of it.
The day should not end
without asking pardon
for any word or deed of ours
that may have hurt or offended others.
Such is what love must be.
When our love is in God and for God,
we free ourselves from
the inconsistent friendship this world promotes.
We love even as we are called to love by Jesus.

LIVING BY GOD'S GRACE

Love as God has loved.

ACKNOWLEDGING GOD'S GIFTS

May this night's rest
refashion my heart through love
so that I may be a loving presence
in every situation, and for everyone.
Forgive my failures of this day, God.
Touch them with your grace
so that the faith and hope of others

may not be shaken by my faults.
Let me not fail to forgive
anyone who may have hurt me.
I don't want anger festering in my heart.
Let me begin anew tomorrow,
with enthusiasm and confidence.
I am convinced about your constant love
and your endless delight in humanity.
I want to be love in this world.
For this day, thank you.
Bless this night.
May tomorrow be a fresh beginning.

Day Seventeen

Jesus called us to love.
It is hard work.
Just as some qualities of life
are an intrinsic part of love,
others work against it.
Love is:
Not arrogant.
So, we are not insensitive to others,
considering ourselves better than them,
and treating them with scorn.
Not selfish.
We do not give only to get,
or think solely of personal benefit.
We do not step on and over others just to be first.
Not negative.
We do not live with endless suspicions,
rash and unfounded judgments,
always assuming the worst of others.
Not harsh.
We do not rejoice at the failure of others,
or at their embarrassment or suffering,
thus neglecting compassion, truth, and justice.

Our growth in love advances
by assuming others' good intentions.
We are becoming truly concerned for others,
and are thus reflecting God
in whose image and likeness we are created.
When we are successful at loving
we should count it as God's grace.
When we fail, we should not be discouraged,
but call upon Jesus to help us.
And he will.

LIVING BY GOD'S GRACE

Ask for the gift of love.

ACKNOWLEDGING GOD'S GIFTS

May this night's rest
be a blessing for me,
recharging my capacity for love
and re-energizing my efforts to love.
Lord, bless this day now closing
with the transforming power of your grace.
May what I did accomplish and attempt
serve as a sign of your loving presence.
Bless the day that will soon begin

with the guidance of your Spirit,
and the power of your Word.
Let tomorrow be another moment
of renewing my commitment
to live as an example of Jesus.
I want to live and love as Jesus did.
For this day, thank you.
Bless this night.
May tomorrow be a fresh beginning.

Day Eighteen

What must we do to become perfect?
Follow Jesus Christ and imitate him.
That's what we promise through baptism;
following Jesus is a consequence of believing him.
Imitating Jesus is a responsibility
and a pathway to happiness.
Jesus came among us
to give us a model for life,
to show us the way to be virtuous.
He said that he was the way by his example,
and the truth by his teaching,
and the life by his death.
This is why Jesus experienced
all that we experience.
He experienced all the stages of human life:
birth, growth, suffering, death.
Each of his actions and his words
gives us something to imitate.
His life is a sure pattern for us,
and a challenge to do what he did,
to make his life a part of ours.
Whatever our disposition,

whatever our life situation,
we can always look to Jesus
and work at imitating him.
That is perfection;
that is the way to salvation.
We turn to Jesus to know and hear
his call, to follow him, to imitate him.
We need, then, to walk in his footsteps,
to live as he lived.

LIVING BY GOD'S GRACE

Walk in the footsteps of Jesus.

ACKNOWLEDGING GOD'S GIFTS

May this night's rest
strengthen my resolve
to live as Jesus lived,
to love as he loved.
Praise to you, God,
for the gift of this day,
for the opportunity and privilege
of living my faith,
of striving to be like Jesus.
When tomorrow dawns, make me alert

to whatever opportunities it will bring.
Give me the grace to be like Jesus
even in the smallest details
of my life and work.
Help me to be faithful.
I want to follow Jesus.
For this day, thank you.
Bless this night.
May tomorrow be a fresh beginning.

Day Nineteen

What is the Christian life?
It is God's life in us through Jesus Christ.
This is a union with Jesus.
This union is as close as possible;
it is his own gift to us.
Imitating Jesus is essential for us,
making us known as Christians.
It has been this way from the beginning.
Thus have Christians always been recognized.
We are so named because of the One we follow.
Jesus is the image of God;
we are called to become the same.
Now, that resemblance will not be seen
unless we show it and live it
through our likeness to Jesus.
There is no other way.
Our Christian life
is about being other Christs.
Jesus' life, presence, and activity
become evident and visible through us.
This is our identity.
Either we take it up,

or we **gradually become invisible.**
The love **of Jesus must be our love** too.
And so too **must be his holiness,**
and compassion, **kindness,**
and forgiveness.
The choice is ours:
to be like Christ
or to be nothing at all.

LIVING BY GOD'S GRACE

Live in the likeness of Jesus.

ACKNOWLEDGING GOD'S GIFTS

May this night's rest
refresh my conviction
and my efforts—big and small—
to live in imitation of Jesus.
Thank you, God, for this day.
Let it be a reminder to me
of all I have done to be like Christ,
and of all that I still need to do.
Tomorrow, I will set out again,
taking each moment as a gift,
and as an invitation to become another Christ.

Give me the grace and desire
to hear that invitation,
however it comes.
I want to be like Jesus.
For this day, thank you.
Bless this night.
May tomorrow be a fresh beginning.

Day Twenty

Jesus Christ should be our model
in all situations, at all times.
Our likeness to him
is the solid foundation
of our journey to eternal glory.
Yes, imitating Jesus is our duty.
It is also our glory,
the glory of one who is called
and chooses to follow.
It is the glory of aiming for
the perfection of the one who is followed.
To some degree,
children recreate the qualities of parents.
Admirers emulate the traits of the admired.
Even if they are not always successful,
their attempts reflect true desire to
become something new.
By calling us to imitate Jesus,
God calls us to a great glory.
Our happiness and our true joy
depend on that imitation,
both now and for eternity.

We are blessed on earth.
We become the recipients of God's love,
insofar as God sees in us,
and in our daily lives and actions,
the very image of Jesus Christ.
At the end of life's journey,
we will be able to claim
the joy of eternal life,
if we are one with Jesus
who lives within us.

LIVING BY GOD'S GRACE

Respond to God's call.

ACKNOWLEDGING GOD'S GIFTS

May this night's rest
provide calm and quiet.
I need calm and quiet to hear God's call,
to accept it, to respond to it,
and to live it.
Forgive the foibles of this passing day.
Forgive me for forgetting or refusing
to listen for the call,
or for failing to act when I did hear it.

Let those mistakes be lessons learned
for whatever the future brings.
Tomorrow will be a new chance for glory,
another gift of time to live the call
with which God has graced me.
May I use that gift wisely, Lord.
I want to know the glory that God promises.
For this day, thank you.
Bless this night.
May tomorrow be a fresh beginning.

Day Twenty-One

There are many ways
to carry out the imitation of Jesus.
All of them can be summed up in a phrase:
"Study Jesus Christ."
When we study him,
we get to know him.
As we come to know him,
we love him.
And because we love him,
we desire and strive to imitate him.
We have to begin with knowing him,
his teaching and his life.
This isn't at all like
knowing the facts and stories
about the life of some celebrity.
This is about love.
We must study and reflect on
the details of the life of Jesus
so that we can know the depth of his love.
We must be filled
with the spirit of his example.
Then, we will come to see

the meaning of his teaching.
We will realize the extent of his mercy.
As we pray for the gift of understanding,
we will begin to know Jesus—truly—
in a profound and practical way.
That knowledge becomes love,
and that love guides us to live as he did,
to be as he was in everything.

Living by God's Grace

Study and know the life of Jesus.

Acknowledging God's Gifts

May this night's rest
clear my mind and heart
of whatever clutter
limits my ability
to examine the life of Jesus
as the model for my own.
Thank you, God,
for the great gift of my faith.
Thank you for the moments in this day
that challenged me to be faithful.
Make up, through your grace,

for those times I failed.
For tomorrow,
let me meet the challenges again.
Support me by the grace of your presence.
I will continue my work
of knowing, loving, and imitating Jesus.
I want to live and love as did Jesus.
For this day, thank you.
Bless this night.
May tomorrow be a fresh beginning.

Day Twenty-Two

Christianity is nothing else
than the life of Jesus Christ
made visible through our behaviors.
Is this possible?
Yes, our spirits can be one with his through faith.
Our hearts can unite with his through love.
And so, our actions can become like his.
But we must be sure
that we have what we need
to excel in this work.
Certainly, we need knowledge
and a focused discipline.
We must work to know ourselves;
we need to know our strengths and weaknesses.
Then we will be well prepared,
ready and willing
to do whatever God asks of us.
We must correct past mistakes, and
that's never an easy task.
Using whatever means are at our disposal,
we can make the present holy,
and so prepare for the future.

Always remember that to succeed in this mission,
we need only to desire it.
A true, strong, and energetic will
is capable of everything.
We strengthen our wills with prayer.
If we spend time in prayer—every day—
we will obtain that strength.
Prayer is a means of grace,
and a key to living as Jesus did.

LIVING BY GOD'S GRACE

Be ready to do whatever God asks.

ACKNOWLEDGING GOD'S GIFTS

May this night's rest
give me the strength
to be faithful to God's work within me,
and open to whatever God may yet do.
Take this day now closing, God,
and all I have done with it,
as a witness of my hope and longing
to be united to you forever.
Tomorrow will bring new adventures
and other possibilities

for growth in faith and love.
Let me take up the adventures
and grasp the possibilities
as a means of knowing myself
and of loving you.
I want to do whatever God asks.
For this day, thank you.
Bless this night.
May tomorrow be a fresh beginning.

Day Twenty-Three

It is of utmost importance
to be attentive
to our everyday activities.
Our destiny for eternity
can be decided—in large part—
by the choices we make in life.
Our holiness is not to be found
in extraordinary accomplishments alone.
If that were the case,
we could stop all our efforts
and declare the spiritual life impossible.
As it is, though,
God finds our holiness
in the little, ordinary acts
we do each day.
This is how we do God's work.
Our life of faith must find its way to our hands.
Then, all our actions are guided by it.
The smallest of our daily tasks
is made holy through our motives
if it is faith that guides them.
When we live our faith like this,

it will be seen clearly
in the desires of our heart,
in the works of our hands,
in the words of our mouth.
Thus, we have a share
in the very holiness of God.
We have cause to be confident—
God will not abandon us.
If we have Jesus, we have everything.

LIVING BY GOD'S GRACE

Be attentive to the little things.

ACKNOWLEDGING GOD'S GIFTS

May this night's rest
make me alert to God
in everyday actions and events,
so that I will not dismiss them
as too ordinary for faith.
Accept my work this day, God,
as the desire to see you,
and to become and live
all that you have called me to be.
Tomorrow will be your gift to me,

another day filled with
all those large and small realities
that hold great potential for holiness.
Give me the grace to do my best
in living my faith with enthusiasm.
I want to be holy.
For this day, thank you.
Bless this night.
May tomorrow be a fresh beginning.

Day Twenty-Four

Jesus himself told us that
his way of life can be reduced to three things:
renouncing ourselves,
taking up the cross,
and walking in his footsteps.
Following Jesus assures us of life with God.
The cross will come for each of us, and we will
have to carry it.
If we follow Jesus and accept the cross,
we will have life.
True life is found in the carrying of this cross,
and nowhere else.
The choice is ours.
We can take up the cross,
but we must also actually carry it,
and carry it courageously.
To drag it along or abandon it
once we begin or after we accept it,
closes us to the graces it holds for us.
We work for holiness and eternal life
by walking the route that Jesus took
on the way to glory and union with God.

This route becomes our own,
and we will find it in our daily lives.
Are we afraid of the struggle?
If we fear it,
we delay coming to the holiness
we so desire and seek.
We turn away from the life promised to us.
The choice is before us.
Will we renounce ourselves, carry our cross, and
follow Jesus?
There is the way to life.

Living by God's Grace

Seek life in the crosses that come.

Acknowledging God's Gifts

May this night's rest
revive within me
the courage and confidence
to carry the crosses
I bear in life.
Lord, I forgive those
who may have been the source
of my crosses this day.

Forgive me for those times
I was a cross to them.
With tomorrow's dawn
will come crosses,
some familiar and some unknown.
Be with me in my efforts
to carry them and learn from them.
I want to grow from the crosses I carry.
For this day, thank you.
Bless this night.
May tomorrow be a fresh beginning.

Day Twenty-Five

Jesus said, "Take up your cross."
What is your cross?
It is many things.
A cross might be the ups and downs of our desires,
our unexamined preferences and expectations.
It can be a materialism that captivates us
with passing things so that we forget eternal truths.
Personal weaknesses can also become a cross.
It's easy to become discouraged, exaggerating
the difficulty of overcoming these weaknesses.
All of this can be a cross.
Human life is like a great Way of the Cross.
We don't have to visit a church
to run through the different stations.
This Way of the Cross is everywhere.
We travel it every day,
even when we are not aware of it.
What can we say to all this?
Simply that there is no other way to heaven.
The cross has its own advantages.
When we carry our crosses,
whatever they may be,

we renounce ourselves.
Even more, we will follow Jesus.
In that following,
we are made holy.
We move ever closer to union with God.
Shouldn't we want to be like the one we follow?
What is your cross?
It is the way to new life.

LIVING BY GOD'S GRACE

Carry the cross; carry your cross.

ACKNOWLEDGING GOD'S GIFTS

May this night's rest
give me the courage
to look within myself
for the cross, the cross meant for me.
I pray for the conviction
to carry the cross I find,
trusting that it can be good for me.
Make up with your grace, Lord,
for any times today
when I avoided the cross
and the transformation it held.

Let me take tomorrow's crosses
without fear or hesitation,
confident that you can draw good from them,
and that they can be blessings for me.
I want to accept whatever crosses come.
For this day, thank you.
Bless this night.
May tomorrow be a fresh beginning.

Day Twenty-Six

Shouldering the cross takes courage.
Only a faith perspective
on the value of the cross
can give us the strength we need.
There is benefit in the cross.
Above all, we learn to see
the advantages of becoming
more and more like the image of Jesus.
By faith, we can see the cross as a treasure,
far more valuable than gold or jewels.
We don't need to look for the cross;
we encounter it every day
in the little events of life.
When we fully accept Christian life,
we learn not to fear our crosses.
They have a transforming power.
Somehow, we develop the courage to receive these crosses
more readily than we would a piece of the true cross.
Don't get beaten down by difficulties,
however hard or heavy they may be.
They are relics of the cross at our fingertips.

Struggles and lack of resources,
betrayal and abandonment by friends,
sickness, the hardships of each day and hour,
the death of loved ones—
all these are the true wood or substance of the cross.
By the cross, we become loving people.
Our love is patient and accepting,
generous and compassionate,
always faithful because it unites us with Christ.
Never forget—
God's help always comes in proportion to our trials.

LIVING BY GOD'S GRACE

Be one with Jesus on the cross.

ACKNOWLEDGING GOD'S GIFTS

May this night's rest
sharpen my awareness
and strengthen my resolve
to accept the crosses I encounter
throughout the day and every day.
Lord, let the crosses I had today,
be the means through which
I continue to grow in your living likeness.

Tomorrow's dawn will bring
both the new and the old,
the familiar and the foreign.
Whatever comes, let it be a call for me
to be patient, compassionate, loving.
I want to live in the likeness of Jesus.
For this day, thank you.
Bless this night.
May tomorrow be a fresh beginning.

Day Twenty-Seven

Jesus will come again.
He has instructed us,
"Watch, because you do not know
when your Lord will return."
We watch and wait
because Jesus will return.
He has promised this.
The one who created us,
brought us to birth,
gave us reason and freedom
will come again.
We need to use our time well
to prepare ourselves as best we can.
Jesus will return as Lord of all,
to examine what we have done
and to decide our future.
We need to think seriously about this.
God's mercy is wide open to us;
grace is extended to us.
Will we accept these gifts?
Can we spend too much time
preparing for the coming of our Lord?

Jesus will return certainly,
but we know neither the year, day, nor hour.
We do not know
how much time remains to us.
What do we have to do to be ready?
How can we use grace well?
"Watch and keep yourselves prepared."
Jesus himself advised us to do this
so we would not be caught napping.

LIVING BY GOD'S GRACE

Think often of the coming of Jesus.

ACKNOWLEDGING GOD'S GIFTS

May this night's rest
inspire and renew my faith,
and make me alert to my hope
that Jesus will come again.
The hours of this day are slipping away.
May they stand as a vigil,
a remembrance of my attentiveness to you.
Let my actions be acceptable to you,
and reflect my desire for you.
For tomorrow, give me confidence.

Help me to prepare myself for a holy life.
Let me be unafraid of my way of life
before the justice and mercy of God.
Since I cannot know the hour,
give me the grace to watch.
I want to be with you, Lord, in time and eternity.
For this day, thank you.
Bless this night.
May tomorrow be a fresh beginning.

Day Twenty-Eight

AWAKENING TO GOD'S PRESENCE

Jesus Christ would have been born in vain
if he didn't renew and develop his life in us
through the gifts of the Holy Spirit.
Those gifts dispose us to listen to the Spirit.
They create a fire burning before us.
These gifts are a strong wind breaking all resistance.
They are electricity circulating through us,
making us reach beyond ourselves,
working with zeal for our holiness
and for the good of others.
Such are the Spirit's gifts at work in us.
Sevenfold are these gifts.
Fear of the Lord to be humble and desire good.
Piety to love God.
Knowledge to discern God's ways.
Courage to do whatever God asks.
Counsel to move always toward God.
Understanding to see the depths of truth.
Wisdom to conform our lives to God's will.
This Spirit transforms our lives
into union with God's own,
without destruction or humiliation,

but by pouring love into us
like a fire that changes all into itself.
So, Jesus Christ lives within us.
We can become new persons,
reproducing in ourselves
his thoughts and sentiments,
his desires, words, and deeds—
in fact, his entire life.
It remains for us to call upon the Spirit.

LIVING BY GOD'S GRACE

Pray for the gifts of the Holy Spirit.

ACKNOWLEDGING GOD'S GIFTS

May this night's rest
open me to the Spirit's lead.
I want to eagerly seek God in my life,
and welcome the fire of God within me.
Thank you, Lord, for the gifts I used today.
Let them be a means of good for others,
reminding them of your presence and your love.
Remind me that my work and efforts
are truly your own.
Come, Holy Spirit, with tomorrow's dawn.

Fashion my heart through love and
teach me anew the ways of Jesus.
Enfold me in your grace;
enchant me so that I might look for no other.
I want to live the Spirit's gifts.
For this day, thank you.
Bless this night.
May tomorrow be a fresh beginning.

Day Twenty-Nine

Jesus has taught us,
"Unless you become like little children,
you will never enter heaven."
But how can we become children again?
How can we be reborn and begin anew?
We can be born again through grace, and
by living the example of Jesus.
The Spirit can fill us with love,
and transform our lives into God's own.
We must live that transformation;
we must live faith, hope, love.
Faith relies not on what the mind reasons,
but believes what is said by those it trusts.
So must we live.
Hope waits in confidence,
without any fear of being disappointed.
So must we live.
Love knows no selfishness;
it works always for the good of others.
This is how we must live.
The life of God is within us.
We have been given a new birth in the divine.

How can we glimpse the depth of this mystery?
We can identify with the Holy Spirit,
with Jesus, and with God.
All this is ours by grace.
We have become completely new beings,
filled with new life.
We participate in God's own nature;
eternal life is our right if our actions merit it.
Give thanks to God, then,
for this capacity to be born again
is truly alive within us.

LIVING BY GOD'S GRACE

Transform life by accepting God's grace.

ACKNOWLEDGING GOD'S GIFTS

May this night's rest
refresh my mind and heart.
I want to be attentive and alert
to the presence of God within me,
and to my call to live in that presence.
As I reflect on the day now passing,
let me see those moments when I missed
or refused God's call and work.

Sharpen my senses for the future.
Tomorrow will bring new opportunities
to believe and hope and love.
I still have opportunities to be transformed,
to live as Jesus lived.
Give me the grace, Lord,
to claim all those opportunities.
I want to transform my life.
For this day, thank you.
Bless this night.
May tomorrow be a fresh beginning.

Day Thirty

"God loved the world so much
that the only Son was given up to death for us."
These words from Jesus explained the great wonder
of God's love for us.
They describe the extravagance of God's love.
This love is a necessary support for our spiritual
journey.
We are given and blessed with other supports.
After Jesus, we can look to Mary.
Mary, too, is capable of such extravagance.
Through love, she gave up that same Son,
for us and for the world.
Mary was tender and loving,
concerned for her Son and concerned for us all.
As the mother of God's Son,
her heart, her love, and her compassion
became a model for Jesus.
He loved her and learned from her.
Who could now measure the extent of her love for us?
Mary journeyed with her Son to Calvary.
There we see her great love for us.
Standing by her Son's cross,

she does what he does.
As he gave himself up for us,
so did she.
After Jesus' own heart,
Mary's heart is the finest masterpiece
to come from the Creator's hands.
Look to Mary, call upon her in confidence.
She will hear us with an open heart
for she is full of compassion and love.

LIVING BY GOD'S GRACE

Look to Mary; call upon her.

ACKNOWLEDGING GOD'S GIFTS

May this night's rest
refashion my heart
to be like Mary's own,
and like her Son's.
Thank you for the gift of this day,
the gift of life and loved ones,
the gift to make a difference in this world.
"Hail, Mary, full of grace."
Gracious God, fill me with grace
and with all I need to live as Jesus did.

"The Lord is with you."
Be ever with me, God,
bless me and guide me—
tomorrow and every day—
in my efforts to do good for others.
I want to be filled and transformed by God's grace.
For this day, thank you.
Bless this night.
May tomorrow be a fresh beginning.

Notes

----

1. The English texts used as a basis for this book are:
   Circular Letters of The Very Reverend Basil Moreau, edited by Joel Gi-allanza, C.S.C., and Jacques Grisé, C.S.C.; Rome: Congregazione di Santa Croce, 1998.

   Personal Letters: sections translated by various religious of Holy Cross as unpublished manuscripts.

   Sermons: *Our Light and Our Way*, translated by Sister M. Eleanore, C.S.C.; Milwaukee: Bruce Publishing Company, 1936.

   Christian Education: translated by Sister Anna Teresa Bayhouse, C.S.C.; Austin: Holy Cross Institute at St. Edward's University, 2006.

   Christian Meditations: translated by a religious of Holy Cross as an unpublished manuscript.

   Catechism of the Christian Life and the Religious Life: sections translated by various religious of Holy Cross as unpublished manuscripts.

   Spiritual Exercises: translated by a religious of Holy Cross as an unpublished manuscript.

2. More information on the ministries of Holy Cross throughout the world can be found in the documents and other resources of the Holy Cross Institute at St. Edward's University (www.holycross institute.org). For additional information on the life and works of Father Moreau, highly recommended reading is *Basil Moreau: Founder of Holy Cross* by Gary MacEoin; revised and updated by Joel Giallanza, C.S.C.; Notre Dame: Ave Maria Press, 2007.

Brother Joel Giallanza, C.S.C., is a member of the South-West Province of the Congregation of Holy Cross and is the author of *Seven Sorrows of Mary*, *Source and Summit*, and *Questions Jesus Asked*. He currently serves as administrative assistant to the provincial of the South-West Province. He is also a spiritual director and offers retreats on continuing formation and the spiritual life.

Founded in 1865, Ave Maria Press,
a ministry of the Congregation of
Holy Cross, is a Catholic publishing
company that serves the spiritual and
formative needs of the Church and its
schools, institutions, and ministers;
Christian individuals and families; and
others seeking spiritual nourishment.

For a complete listing of titles from

Ave Maria Press

Sorin Books

Forest of Peace

Christian Classics

visit www.avemariapress.com

ave maria press® / Notre Dame, IN 46556
A Ministry of the United States Province of Holy Cross